First World War
and Army of Occupation
War Diary
France, Belgium and Germany

38 DIVISION
Divisional Troops
D Squadron 1/1 Wiltshire Yeomanry
4 December 1915 - 21 April 1916

WO95/2545/1

The Naval & Military Press Ltd
www.nmarchive.com
Published in association with The National Archives

Published by

The Naval & Military Press Ltd

Unit 10 Ridgewood Industrial Park,

Uckfield, East Sussex,

TN22 5QE England

Tel: +44 (0) 1825 749494

www.naval-military-press.com

www.nmarchive.com

This diary has been reprinted in facsimile from the original. Any imperfections are inevitably reproduced and the quality may fall short of modern type and cartographic standards.

© **Crown Copyright**
Images reproduced by permission of The National Archives, London, England, 2015.

Contents

Document type	Place/Title	Date From	Date To
Heading	WO95/2545/1		
Heading	38th Division 'D' Sqdn 1-1st Wilts Yeo Dec 1915-Apr 1916 To 15 Corps		
Heading	D Sq. Wilts Yeo Vol. 3		
Heading	D Sq 1/1 Wilts Yeo Vol I & II 38th D.T.		
War Diary	Havre	04/12/1915	04/12/1915
War Diary	Blendecques	05/12/1915	05/12/1915
War Diary	Enguingatte	20/12/1915	20/12/1915
War Diary	Les Amusoires (St Venant)	25/01/1916	25/01/1916
War Diary		15/01/1916	15/01/1916
War Diary	Paradis	29/02/1916	29/02/1916
War Diary		17/01/1916	17/01/1916
War Diary		23/02/1916	23/02/1916
War Diary	Paradis	01/03/1916	01/03/1916
War Diary	Hinges	03/03/1916	04/04/1916
War Diary	Lagorgue	21/04/1916	21/04/1916

woas/2545/1

38TH DIVISION

'D' SQDN 1-1ST WILTS YEO

DEC 1915-APR 1916

To 15 Corps

"D" Sq. Diets ⁹⁄₆₀
vol: 3

1915
"D" Sp: 1/1 Wilts Yeo:
Vots I & II
38th D.T.

Dec '15
Ap '16

Army Form C. 2118

1/1 Royal Wilts Yeomanry (380th)
In the Field

WAR DIARY
or
INTELLIGENCE SUMMARY
(Erase heading not required.)

Instructions regarding War Diaries and Intelligence Summaries are contained in F.S. Regs., Part II. and the Staff Manual respectively. Title Pages will be prepared in manuscript.

Place	Date	Hour	Summary of Events and Information	Remarks and references to Appendices
	Dec. 1915			
HAVRE.	4.	8:30am	H.Qrs. M.Gun Sec. & "D" Sqdn. 1/1st Royal Wilts Yeo. disembarked.	
		3:30pm	Entrained & proceeded to BLENDECQUES, reaching there 3:30pm 5.12.15	
BLENDECQUES.	5.	4:30pm	Marched into billets at ENGUINGATTE, 6:30pm	
ENGUINGATTE	20.	8:30am	Marched from ENGUINGATTE to LES AMUSIORES (ST. VENANT) into billets. (Reserve Area)	
	3.12.15 to 31.12.15		OPERATIONS
NIL.

TRAINING.
The C.O., 2nd in Command, Squadron Leader, & 3 Troops of each Sqdn. were attached, separately, to Guards Division in the front line trenches for instruction in trench routine. | |

A.G. Thynne
Major.
Comdg. 1/1. R. Wilts Yeomanry

Army Form C. 2118

WAR DIARY
or
INTELLIGENCE SUMMARY
(Erase heading not required.)

1/4 Royal Wilts Yeomanry (38th Div)
Lt. Col. Selfe

Instructions regarding War Diaries and Intelligence Summaries are contained in F. S. Regs., Part II. and the Staff Manual respectively. Title Pages will be prepared in manuscript.

Place	Date	Hour	Summary of Events and Information	Remarks and references to Appendices
LES AMUSOIRES. (ST VENANT)	25.1.16	9 am	Marched into billets at PARADIS. (Forward area) S. of MERVILLE.	
			OPERATIONS.	
			NIL.	
			TRAINING	
			Remaining Troop & Divl. Squadron was attached to 113th Brigade in the front line for instruction in Trench routine.	
	15.1.16		Lt. Col. U. O. THYNNE. D.S.O. left to assume command of 8th Batt. Rifle Brigade.	

A. G. Thynne
Major
Comdg. 1/1. R. Wilts Yeomanry

Army Form C. 2118

13/3

WAR DIARY
or
INTELLIGENCE SUMMARY
(Erase heading not required.)

1/1 Royal Bucks Yeomanry

H.Q. DIVISIONAL MOUNTED TROOPS
38th DIVISION

Instructions regarding War Diaries and Intelligence Summaries are contained in F.S. Regs., Part II. and the Staff Manual respectively. Title Pages will be prepared in manuscript.

Place	Date	Hour	Summary of Events and Information	Remarks and references to Appendices
PARADIS.	29.2.16.		Operations. Nil.	
			Training.	
	17.1.16		Machine Gun Section, R.W.Y. was attached for instruction to the Machine Gun Coy. Guards Division in the Trenches.	
	23.2.16.		Lt.Col. U.O Thynne D.S.O. returned & assumed command of Div.l Mounted Troops.	
			Major Lord A.G Thynne left to assume duties of 2nd in Command, 10th Bt Worcestershire Regt.	

Wm Thynne
Lt Colonel
Commdg 1/1 Royal Bucks Y/o

Addendum to Cav Sect
Letter

WAR DIARY or INTELLIGENCE SUMMARY

1/Royal Welsh Fus
D Wells Yeo
XXXVIII
Vol 4

Place	Date	Hour	Summary of Events and Information	Remarks and references to Appendices
PARADIS.	1.3.16.		Marches to HINGES into new billets.	
HINGES	3.3.16.		Operations. Nil.	
			Duty. Machine Gun Section Royal Welsh Yeomanry furnishes 2 machine Guns in front line trenches.	

E.P. North B. Reid.
Connels. S. Gordon.
1/ R. Welsh Yeomanry

XXXVIII Army Form C. 2118
vol #5.

WAR DIARY
or
INTELLIGENCE SUMMARY
(Erase heading not required.)

Place	Date	Hour	Summary of Events and Information	Remarks and references to Appendices
HINGES	1/4/16		Training	
	4/4/16		H.Q. & 1½ Squadron of R.W.Y. marched to B Isques, Pas de Calais for a fortnight Swimming course 1st Cavalry Division.	
LA GORGUE	21/4/16		Returned from Swimming and moved into new billets at LA GORGUE. Operations Nil.	

S.P.S.H.P. Lieut.
Comm'g Lt-Col 1st R.Wilts Yeomanry
30/4/16.

www.ingramcontent.com/pod-product-compliance
Lightning Source LLC
Chambersburg PA
CBHW081254170426
43191CB00037B/2157